taste & see™

Life is Sweet

BAKING DEVOTIONS FOR KIDS

by Ruthanne VandenBosch

Warner Press, Inc
Warner Press and "WP" logo are trademarks of Warner Press, Inc

Taste and See™
Life Is Sweet: Baking Devotions for Kids
Written by Ruthanne VandenBosch

Copyright ©2014 Warner Press Inc

Requests for information should be sent to:
Warner Press Inc
1201 East Fifth Street
P.O. Box 2499
Anderson, IN 46012
www.warnerpress.org

Editors: Robin Fogle and Karen Rhodes
Designers: Curtis Corzine and Christian Elden

ISBN: 978-1-59317-751-5

Printed in USA

TABLE OF CONTENTS

1.....................5

EASY   MORE DIFFICULT

Special thanks to Paul Armstrong—navy chaplain, mentor, and friend—for reviewing each lesson and reminding me that while God's standards are important to teach, it is relationship with Him that should cause us to obey. Thank you, Paul!

Introduction:

Hello, and welcome to "Life Is Sweet," a dessert cookbook for kids, with a twist.

Each of the twelve recipes included in this book are accompanied by a Bible lesson. The lesson ties directly to the recipe, using ingredients, techniques, and even taste-testing to teach biblical truths like: grace, keeping a pure heart, being obedient, using your gifts, and characteristics of God.

Maybe you are a parent or grandparent, wanting to spend time in the kitchen with your kids or grandkids. Maybe you are a Sunday school teacher, pastor, or missionary, wanting to reach kids in your church with the Good News of God's love in a new and different way. Maybe you are a college student with a neighborhood full of kids around you, and you are wondering how you can reach them for Jesus. Whoever you are, if you are looking for a fun, new way to teach about God, this is it!

Each recipe in this book includes:

- An ingredient list.
- Tips for preparing ahead.
- Directions that include step-by-step pictures.
- A lesson that teaches something about living for God.
- Questions to spark discussion about what was learned.

Kids are so excited to learn new things, and with all of the "baking competition" style shows on TV lately, this is a *great* way to share a useful skill along with biblical truth. Whether you decide to bake at home or host a class in your church kitchen, the boys and girls in your life are going to love this approach to learning about God.

Getting Started:

The recipes in this book are arranged in a specific order:

1. Basic understanding of God
2. Presentation of the Gospel
3. How to grow in your walk with God

The lessons can be done out of this order, but if you have children who don't know God, it might be helpful to follow it.

The lessons also are rated in difficulty from one (easy) to five (more difficult). If you have beginning bakers, you might arrange your lessons in order of difficulty.

To begin a lesson, plan ahead a few days before you meet.
- Read through the entire recipe and lesson.
- Check for ingredients you need and equipment you might not have.
- Read the lesson and think about each child who will come.
- Pray about how to best discuss the lesson and think about how the kids might answer each question.

- Decide when, during the recipe, you will do your lesson. Sometimes it is best to do the lesson while the recipe bakes, sometimes while it cools, and sometimes it is best to finish baking completely before doing the lesson.

The day of the lesson, prepare what you will need.
- Prepare ingredients ahead if needed (like getting butter or cream cheese to room temperature).
- Get all of your ingredients ready and think about what jobs the kids can be a part of. If you have a large group, think about how to divide up jobs equally so no one gets bored.
- Think about safety. Are supplies and equipment set up so kids will be able to reach them? Are surfaces clean and extra paper towels available? Are there special instructions you will need to give for equipment like electric beaters?

When the kids arrive:
- Tell parents you will need about 2 hours, depending on the recipe.
- Welcome them and talk about what you will be making and what the whole process looks like.
- Talk about kitchen safety. Pull long hair back, scrub hands well, teach about oven and microwave safety, and discuss any kitchen equipment that will be used.
- Put the recipe together. Allow the kids to measure, stir, and take part in all parts of the recipe.
- Give help with things like using a mixer or removing items from a hot oven, especially if you are working with younger kids.
- Sit down with the kids and go through the lesson. Encourage questions and interaction. Pray with your group.
- Enjoy eating your dessert together!

The recipes in this book are tried and true, but sometimes a recipe can go wrong. If that happens, don't panic! You have a great opportunity to talk about second chances! We don't always get things right the first time, but God always gives us a second chance. Invite them back for a different recipe and lesson the next week.

As I worked on this book, I have been praying for you! I have been praying that the person who opens this book with the desire to teach little ones about Jesus would be blessed. I pray that God uses these recipes and lessons to open doors for you to share the love of God with the children in your life. I pray the Holy Spirit brings understanding and hope to you and to the young lives you will touch.

God Bless!

Ruthanne

P.S. Make sure you check out the video at http://warnerpress.org/books/lifeissweet/

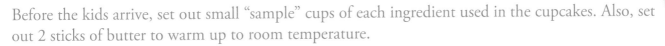

FUDGE CUPCAKES *with* BUTTER CREAM ICING

Theme: Trusting that God works everything together for good

Before the kids arrive, set out small "sample" cups of each ingredient used in the cupcakes. Also, set out 2 sticks of butter to warm up to room temperature.

Who likes cupcakes? I think cupcakes are my favorite dessert. I like picking out fun cupcake papers and pretty sprinkles for the top! Today we are going to make chocolate cupcakes with vanilla icing. Before you start, you will be asked to taste-test all of the ingredients. I've left a spot next to each ingredient for you to write a ONE WORD description of what you think about that ingredient's flavor (Yum, Yuck, Nasty, Tasty…be creative!)

Give each kid a list of the ingredients and a pencil. (You can make your own list or photocopy the one in the back of the book.) Have the kids taste a little of each ingredient and write one word to describe each. Have fun discussing the tastes together before you start baking.

> **Prep Time:** 15 minutes **Bake Time:** 20 minutes **Cool/Frost Time:** 20 minutes

Cupcake Ingredients: (Makes 12 cupcakes)

- 1 ½ cups flour
- 1 cup sugar
- ¼ cup cocoa powder
- ½ teaspoon salt
- 1 teaspoon baking soda
- 1 tablespoon white vinegar
- ½ teaspoon vanilla
- ⅓ cup vegetable oil
- 1 cup water

Icing Ingredients:

- 2 sticks (one cup) butter, at room temperature.
- 1 ½ cups powdered sugar
- 1 teaspoon vanilla

Getting Started:

- **Check your ingredients list to make sure you have everything you need.**
- **Place 12 cupcake liners into a cupcake or muffin tin.**
- **Preheat oven to 350° F.**

NOW YOU ARE READY TO BAKE!

Cupcake Steps:

- Place all dry ingredients into a large mixing bowl and stir together until well blended.
- Add all the liquid ingredients to the dry and stir until smooth.
- Divide batter equally into cupcake liners. I use a scoop to do this, but you can use a spoon. Fill each liner about ⅔ full.
- Bake at 350° F for 20-25 minutes.
- Remove from oven, and when cupcakes are cool enough to touch, remove them from pan and let them cool on the counter.
- Make buttercream icing while they cool.

Icing Steps:

- Place all ingredients in a large mixing bowl.
- Use a mixer to beat ingredients together on low speed. This can be very messy! You might want to help the kids the first time you do this.)
- Once ingredients are combined, mix on high for 1 to 2 minutes, scraping sides with a spatula, until very light and fluffy.
- Frost cupcakes with a knife, or pipe frosting on, using a decorating tip.

  (To see how to pipe frosting, visit http://warnerpress.org/books/lifeissweet/ for an instructional video.)

- Add sprinkles!

Lesson:

Let's talk about those ingredients you just tried.

(Let kids discuss answers to the taste-test and share your thoughts on the flavors.)

- Which ingredients were your favorite?
- Which were your least favorite?
- If you could pick one ingredient to eat a whole bowl of, what would it be?
- Did most of the ingredients taste good or bad?

I think the only things that tasted good were the sugar and the water. I think everything else was pretty gross, especially the vinegar!

- Since we are using mostly yucky-tasting ingredients, do you think the cupcakes will be good?

You'll have to try them for yourselves once they are finished baking, but I think they are really yummy chocolate cupcakes!

- How do you think this happens?

(Just let them speculate. Depending on your group and time frame you could look up reasons for adding things like flour and baking soda to a cake.)

Today we are going to talk about a big word: *sovereignty.*

- Have you ever heard this word before? Do you know what it means?

The dictionary definition is "supreme power or authority."

God is described as being sovereign. This means that He has the final say in absolutely everything. Sometimes this characteristic of God is confusing to people. If God has the final say in everything, then why do bad things happen to me? Does that make God evil or mean?

These cupcakes can help us understand this characteristic of God. Think of all those yucky ingredients as bad things that happen in life.

- What are some bad things that have happened in your life?

(Let kids just talk here—be especially sensitive to the wide range of experience. For some kids the worst thing ever is getting a "B" in a class and for others they lost a parent to cancer. Try to not minimize the "small" things.)

Maybe you got really sick, or your parents got a divorce, or your best friend found a new best friend and left you.

Lots of really hard things happen to us. There are a lot of reasons why they happen. Sometimes they happen because another person does something to hurt us, sometimes they just happen (like getting sick) and we don't know why.

The important thing to understand about God is that He can do something AMAZING with the bad things that happen, if we let Him.

Just like all the different (mostly yucky) ingredients combine together to make yummy cupcakes, God can take everything in our lives—all the bad *and* all the good—and make it beautiful.

Here's what the Bible says:

(If time permits, you can pass out Bibles and show the kids how to look up the verses.)

Romans 8:28 (ESV): *And we know that for those who love God all things work together for good, for those who are called according to His purpose.*

- There is a requirement in this verse—what is it?

- Do you meet this requirement?

- If not, will you ask your leader more about how to love God?

Ecclesiastes 3:11 (NIV): *He has made everything beautiful in its time. He has also set eternity in the human heart; yet no one can fathom what God has done from beginning to end.*

In its time…

This means that bad things might continue to look bad for a while. When we love God and trust in His promises, we look forward to the day when even the bad things in our lives are made into something beautiful.

2 Corinthians 5:7 (NIV): *For we live by faith, not by sight.*

You trusted that I knew what I was doing when I told you all those yucky ingredients would make a good cupcake. You went ahead and put them together and put them in the oven.

Now, as you go frost and eat those cupcakes, I want you to think about how you can better love and trust God. When you trust Him, you will believe that *somehow* He will work ALL things together for good in your life.

And He will!

Pray:

Pray with kids before finishing recipe—or later before you eat cupcakes. Ask God to help them love and trust Him more.

UGLY COOKIES
Theme: *God sees who you are inside*

Today we are going to make some special cookies. They are different from the usual sort of cookie because they have something hidden inside. A *treasure*. This recipe asks you to put Hershey Hugs® inside, but there are lots of candies you could add to the middle of these cookies. Mini Reese's Peanut Butter Cups® are good or Mini Snickers®. You can have a lot of fun experimenting with this recipe.

> **Prep Time:** 35 minutes **Bake Time:** 10 minutes **Decorating Time:** 15 minutes

The time involved here is totally dependant on how many little hands you have helping out! This is a great hands-on recipe for kids. They can help unwrap all of the candy and "hide" the candy inside each cookie.

Cookie Ingredients: (Makes about 30-40 small cookies)

- **1 bag (approx. 40) Hershey Hugs®**
- **1 box (8 oz.) cream cheese**
- **1 bag (12 oz.) semi-sweet chocolate chips**
- **2 cups all-purpose flour**

Icing Ingredients:

- **Wilton® chocolate candy melts (1 bag)**
- **Wilton® white chocolate candy melts (1 bag)**

Getting Started:

- **Check your ingredient list to make sure you have everything you need.**
- **Preheat oven to 350° F.**
- **Cut parchment paper to fit on each of your cookie sheets.**

NOW YOU ARE READY TO BAKE!

Cookie Steps:

- Unwrap all of your Hershey Hugs® and put them in a small bowl.
- Soften cream cheese in microwave. Stir until it is completely smooth.
- Melt chocolate chips in microwave for 30 seconds and stir. Repeat this until all of the chocolate chips are melted and smooth.
- Add cream cheese and melted chocolate together in a large bowl and mix well.
- Add flour and stir into a thick dough consistency. You can use clean hands to knead the dough at the end until all of the flour is mixed in.
- Measure out one tablespoon of dough, roll it into a ball, and place it in the center of your hand.
- Flatten dough out by pressing on it with your other hand.
- Place one Hershey Hug® in the center and gently push dough around the entire candy until it is covered.

Kids might need a little help and practice here. Show them how to do this and then help. It's a little harder with small hands.

- Roll cookie into a ball and place on a parchment paper-covered cookie sheet.
- Bake cookies at 350°F for 8-10 minutes.
- Remove cookies from oven and slide parchment paper (with cookies on top) onto counter to cool.

Have the lesson at this point, or at the end. Be sure to take a good look at how ugly these cookies are before they are decorated

Icing Steps:

- To decorate, melt about 1 cup of white chocolate and ½ cup of dark chocolate (use a candy-making kind of chocolate so that it hardens quickly and smoothly—I use Wiltons®) in the microwave. Heat it for 30 seconds, stir it, and repeat until all chocolate is melted.
- Dip ½ of each cooled cookie in the white chocolate and place them on a clean sheet of parchment paper to harden.

You can speed up the process by placing the parchment paper on a cookie sheet first, and once they are decorated, putting the cookies in the refrigerator for a few minutes to harden.

- Place melted dark chocolate into a small zip-top bag and clip off a *tiny* corner.
- Carefully drizzle the chocolate back and forth over the whole cookie top.

Lesson:

These are really ugly cookies, don't you think? Have you decorated them yet? Get a good look at them before you do. Little brown blobs…kind of dry and cracked looking. If you went into a bakery and looked into the glass case and you could choose anything inside—creamy cupcakes, giant chocolate chip cookies, slices of layer cake—would you pick one of these? I definitely would *not*.

We judge the world around us by what we see. If something is pretty, cool, colorful, fun, or entertaining, we judge it as good. If something is ugly, smelly, or boring, we judge it as bad, or maybe even worthless.

(You can stop here and talk about some of these things if time permits.)

If we judge these cookies only by what they look like right out of the oven, we would have to say they are terrible cookies.

We are going to judge these cookies by something else though—not just by what we see, but by what we KNOW. We KNOW that there's a treasure inside. We are going to take the time to decorate these cookies so that the outside is a reflection of what is inside.

- What if we had filled the cookies with liver? We could throw them in the trash now, right?

- What if we decorated those liver-filled cookies really pretty? Would that make them better?

- What is more important: what the cookie looks like, or what is inside the cookie?

The Bible tells a story about some people who made themselves look good on the outside but were as nasty as liver on the inside.

In the days when Jesus was here on earth, there were men called Pharisees. They made lots of rules for people and did lots of things to make everyone think they were really good people. It was really important to them for everyone to see how good they were. It was also really important to them that they got recognition and rewards for doing good things. They loved "looking good" to others more than they loved God.

Jesus talks about them in the book of Matthew, chapter 23. He says to them:
You clean the outside of the cup and dish, but inside they are full of greed and self-indulgence. Blind Pharisee! First clean the inside of the cup and dish, and then the outside also will be clean (verses 25-26, NIV).

My dishwasher doesn't always work very well. Sometimes when I go to grab a mug for coffee or cocoa I will look and see food stuck to the inside. Yuck. The outside looks clean, but it's not really the outside that is important here. I don't want my drink to have little pieces of food floating in it. The inside matters.

Jesus is telling these men that it doesn't matter how popular or handsome or spiritual they are on the outside; He is saying it's what is INSIDE that counts.

God knows what is inside of you. The Bible says, *People look at the outward appearance, but the Lord looks at the heart* (1 Samuel 16:7, NIV). No matter how "good" or "bad" you look to others, God knows your heart. He knows why you do what you do.

• Do you sometimes care more about what people think of you than what God thinks about you?

• Why do you think that is?

• How do you think you would go about "cleaning the inside of the cup?"

(Discuss this and explain that to do this you have to be honest and really look at the reason you are doing something. You need to be willing to listen to what God has to say. Sadly, the Pharisees didn't listen to Jesus and missed having a treasure on the inside.

Explain that it is really helpful to look for someone you respect, who is more mature in his or her faith [like parents or Sunday School teachers], and ask that person to help you as you take a look at the "inside of the cup.")

Here are some steps that might help you "clean out your cup":

1. **Pray and ask God to help you see your heart. Allow God to search it and tell you what needs to be cleaned out.**

God knows your heart—even if you don't want Him to know it—but many times we don't want to hear what He has to say about it.

When you are doing something wrong, God will give you a conviction (or a strong feeling) that it is wrong. He might use the Bible to give you that feeling when you read something and realize you need to change, or He might use another person to help you see that what you are doing is wrong. When we see someone else hurt by our actions or when a person we respect points something out, we should listen. It might be God telling us to clean out our heart.

(Kids can look up the verses that follow and read them aloud if time permits.)

Search me, God, and know my heart; test me and know my anxious thoughts. See if there is any offensive way in me, and lead me in the way everlasting. Psalm 139:23-24 (NIV)

2. **Start paying attention to things that show your "insides" to the world around you. One indication of how your heart is doing is what words come out of your mouth. When your words start sounding negative and harsh, go back to step one and ask God to show you what needs to be cleaned out.**

A good man brings good things out of the good stored up in his heart, and an evil man brings evil things out of the evil stored up in his heart. For the mouth speaks what the heart is full of. Luke 6:45 (NIV)

3. **Ask God to clean your heart and help you to keep it clean. Once you know of an area in your life that needs to be cleaned out, you can take action by praying for help. God is always willing to help us. The hard part is obeying Him once you know what He wants you to do. A good example is gossiping. If you are in the habit of talking badly about others or sharing information that should be kept secret, God will want to help you stop this. It might be hard at first, when you have something you REALLY want to say, but shouldn't. Remember, God is with you and will help you obey.**

Asking someone else who follows God to help you follow through in cleaning up is a very smart thing to do. It is important that you give that person permission to hold you accountable. In other words, he or she gets to ask if you are changing in your problem area. That person can also help when you feel tempted. Often times, just texting a quick note, asking him or her to pray for you can help out a lot. The bottom line is you don't have to do this step alone.

Create in me a clean heart, O God; and renew a right spirit within me. Psalm 51:10 (NIV)

If you have decided to follow Jesus, these steps toward keeping a clean heart are steps you will follow your entire life. Sometimes it can be hard, but paying attention to what's inside of your heart and keeping it clean will honor God and bring you so many benefits.

Pray:

As we enjoy these cookies together, let's think about the difference between what we can see on the outside and what actually exists on the inside. Let's ask God to help us to care more about what's inside of us than what we look like on the outside.

Cinnamon Cheesecake Sundaes
Theme: God created you with unique gifts and abilities

When you make an ice cream sundae, you begin with a scoop of plain ice cream in a cup or a bowl. It doesn't really look all that exciting. What makes the sundae special is all the delicious toppings you add to it. Every sundae is as unique as the person who made it. Today we are going to make sundaes—but not the kind with ice cream. We are going to make mini cinnamon cups filled with a scoop of cheesecake filling. Then you can top them with all of your favorite things! Be creative!!

Prep Time: 20 minutes **Bake Time:** 8 minutes **Decorating Time:** 10 minutes

Note: Put whipped topping in the refrigerator the night before you make these and take cream cheese out of the fridge about an hour before the kids arrive.

This lesson will illustrate creativity, so the greater variety of toppings you can provide, the better. If you have a bulk section in your grocery, you can get just a bit of several candies and toppings. A big favorite for this age group is gummy candies.

Ingredients:

(Makes 12 cinnamon cheesecake sundaes)

- **12 wonton wrappers (usually found in produce section of grocery)**
- **1 cup granulated sugar (divided)**
- **1 teaspoon cinnamon**
- **Non-stick cooking spray**
- **1 (8 oz.) package cream cheese (at room temperature)**
- **1 teaspoon vanilla**
- **1 (8 oz.) tub whipped topping (thawed in refrigerator overnight)**
- **Any sundae toppings you like**
- **A variety of chopped candies or cookies to use as toppings**

Sundae Cups Steps:

- Preheat oven to 350° F.
- Mix ½ cup of sugar with cinnamon and put on a small plate.
- Lightly spray both sides of one wonton wrapper with cooking spray and lay it in the cinnamon and sugar mixture. Once one side is coated, turn it over and coat the other side.
- Place cinnamon covered wrapper into an ungreased muffin tin, pushing the center down to form a little cup.
- Do this with a total of 12 wrappers, filling each cavity in the muffin tin.
- Bake at 350° F for about 8 minutes, until golden brown on edges. Check often.
- Remove from oven and carefully pick each cup out of the muffin tin and place on a plate to cool completely.

Cheesecake Filling:

- Cream together remaining sugar with room temperature cream cheese.
- Add vanilla and combine completely.
- Fold in ½ of the tub of whipped topping and stir until smooth.
- When cups are cool, spoon or scoop filling evenly into each cup.
- Decorate using remaining whipped topping and any other toppings you like.

Note: Let your bakers go crazy making their own sundae to eat while you finish the others. I used hot fudge sauce, whipped topping, confetti sprinkles, and a red Sixlets® candy on top.

Lesson:

There are a lot of things that have to be done the same way every time—like brushing your teeth. There aren't too many creative things you can do with brushing your teeth. You can get a fun toothbrush or bubblegum flavored toothpaste, but you basically have to stand at the sink and brush and rinse.

Not everything needs to be done the same way every time though. I love it when I'm given the freedom to be creative!

- Did you enjoy being creative with these sundaes?

- What did you put on your own personal sundae?

I put fudge, caramel, coconut, and M&Ms® on mine! YUM!

Maybe you didn't have everything you needed to make your "perfect" sundae.

- If you could have had anything in the world to add to your sundae, what would it have been?

- When you shared your "perfect" creations with each other, did anyone have the exact same creation as another person in the group?

Probably not! Maybe some of them were similar, but I bet you each thought up pretty unique combinations.

Why is this? Because we are created by God to be totally unique! Even identical twins are unique. I have cousins, Scott and Steve, who are identical. I asked them what *they* would add to a sundae.

Scott: *hot fudge, bananas, whipped cream with chocolate drizzled over the whipped cream*

Steve: *hot fudge, chocolate, Reese's Pieces®, M&Ms®, and Oreos®*

Even twins are completely different in some ways!

God has not only created each of us to be unique, He has given each of us specific gifts and abilities to be used for Him.

- Can you think of any unique gifts or abilities that you have? (Give kids time to respond.)

Maybe you can play an instrument or read really well. Maybe you are a good listener or able to speak in front of groups without being afraid. Maybe you are good at art or at understanding numbers.

The Bible says, *Each of you should use whatever gift you have received to serve others, as faithful stewards of God's grace in its various forms* (1 Peter 4:10, NIV). Everyone has been given special abilities and talents by God, and one ability or talent is not better or more important than another.

Sometimes we believe the wrong things about this—things like:

"I have really important talents and that makes me better than other people."

"I don't have any talents. Everyone is better than me at everything."

"That person has no talents at all. He or she is worthless."

"I have talents, but they are dumb talents. I want talents like so-and-so."

All of these things are **NOT** true.

God gives each person the perfect gifts and abilities for him or her. No ability or gift is more important than any other. They all are important, and they all work together to make us a team.

Who is the most important person on a football team? Maybe the quarterback?

Some of the players have the most visible positions, but without the offensive line, they would be sacked on every single play. Plus, who would run the ball? Who would catch it? Who would kick the extra point?

What about the defense? If the only person on defense was the quarterback, the opposing team would score on every single drive. There would be no way to stop them.

The Bible talks about gifts and abilities in 1 Corinthians 12:14-27 (NIV). (If you like, you can photocopy the scripture located in the back of this book, cut it apart, and let each child read a section.)

These verses relate each person and their abilities to a part of the body:

Even so the body is not made up of one part but of many. Now if the foot should say, "Because I am not a hand, I do not belong to the body," it would not for that reason stop being part of the body. And if the ear should say, "Because I am not an eye, I do not belong to the body," it would not for that reason stop being part of the body. If the whole body were an eye, where would the sense of hearing be? If the whole body were an ear, where would the sense of smell be? But in fact God has placed the parts in the body, every one of them, just as he wanted them to be. If they were all one part, where would the body be? As it is, there are many parts, but one body.

The eye cannot say to the hand, "I don't need you!" And the head cannot say to the feet, "I don't need you!" On the contrary, those parts of the body that seem to be weaker are indispensable, and the parts that we think are less honorable we treat with special honor. And the parts that are unpresentable are treated with special modesty, while our presentable parts need no special treatment. But God has put the body together, giving greater honor to the parts that lacked it, so that there should be no division in the body, but that its parts should have equal concern for each other. If one part suffers, every part suffers with it; if one part is honored, every part rejoices with it. Now you are the body of Christ, and each one of you is a part of it.

Describe what these verses are saying about gifts and abilities.

- What happens if we think our gifts or others' gifts are better than others?

- What happens if we think our gifts or others' gifts are unimportant?

- What are some ways you could use your gifts and abilities for God?

- What are some ways you could help your friends use their gifts and abilities for God?

(Spend some time thinking of specific gifts for each person in your group. Think of some ways that each person can use them this week for God's glory. Maybe some of your gifts even work together!)

Pray:

Pray for each other to discover and use your abilities for God. Ask God to help you see worth and value in all the people around you, even if it seems like they don't have much to offer.

STRAWBERRY CREAM COOKIES

Theme: *God's gift of grace/salvation*

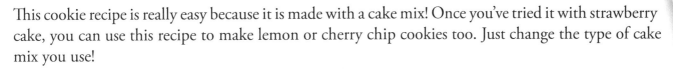

This cookie recipe is really easy because it is made with a cake mix! Once you've tried it with strawberry cake, you can use this recipe to make lemon or cherry chip cookies too. Just change the type of cake mix you use!

You will want to do a few things to prepare for this lesson. Your bakers will be giving away all of these cookies, so try to have a plan ahead of time for who you will be giving them to. If you have a small group, you can travel with the cookies; otherwise, ask a neighbor if you could stop by for a few minutes with some kids and some cookies.

Also, take your cream cheese and margarine out of the refrigerator about an hour before your bakers arrive.

Prep Time: 10 minutes *Baking Time:* 12-15 minutes

Ingredients:

- 1 box strawberry cake mix
- ⅓ cup margarine (soft, at room temperature)
- ½ box (4 ounces) cream cheese (soft, at room temperature)
- 1 bag white chocolate chips
- 1 egg

Directions:

- Preheat oven to 350° F.
- Cover 2 cookie sheets with parchment paper.
- Cream together margarine and cream cheese until smooth.
- Add egg, stirring until smooth.
- Melt ⅓ cup of white chocolate chips and stir in.
- Add cake mix and stir until combined. Use clean hands to knead mixture into a heavy cookie dough.
- Add remaining white chocolate chips and combine well.
- Make evenly-sized, small balls of dough using a spoon or a cookie scoop.
- Place on a parchment paper-covered cookie sheet, leaving room for cookies to spread as they bake.
- Bake at 350° F for 12-14 minutes.
- Remove from oven, slide parchment paper (cookies and all!) onto a clean counter to cool.

Lesson:

Today we are going to talk about being fair.

- Who thinks that things should always be fair?

- Can you think of something recently that happened to you that wasn't fair?

(Give kids time to respond to the questions.)

I remember a lot of stuff that happened when my brother and I were little that wasn't fair. He got to sit in the best seat in the car. He got to choose first. He didn't have to do as many chores. I had long lists of how unfair things were.

As I grew up, things were still unfair. I didn't get the classes I wanted at school. I had to work the weekend hours at my job, while other people got to have the weekends off because their parents were friends with the boss. I couldn't get the super-expensive, brand-name clothes I wanted because my parents wouldn't let me.

A few minutes ago, we made cookies together, and now I think we should figure out together the fairest way of dividing them up.

- Who provided the kitchen you made them in?

- Whose bowls, pans, and oven did you use?

- Who paid for the ingredients?

- Who spent the time and gas to go to the store and get the ingredients?

So…who deserves the cookies? Should I get *all* of the cookies?

You might argue that you actually helped in the *making* of the cookies. So maybe you deserve a percentage of the total number of cookies.

- How many cookies did you make in total?

- How many do you think would be fair to give to someone who really only helped mix the ingredients?

Let's come to a decision on the number of cookies each person involved should get if we were to be perfectly fair.

- Does everyone agree that this decision is fair?

OK.

Now, your cookies should be cool. Let's go back into the kitchen and find a pretty plate. I want you to put all of the cookies on the plate and wrap them up, and then we'll go find someone to give them to.

ALL of them.

When we get back from our visit, we can finish this lesson.

- How did giving away all the cookies feel?
- Was it hard to do something that was so obviously unfair?

We have a word for this: **grace**.

One meaning for the word grace is "unmerited favor." This means that we are given something we did not earn or deserve.

- Who deserved the cookies?
- Who got the cookies?

That person was shown grace. He or she got cookies that person did not deserve.

God gives us grace like this too. When we allow God to come into our lives and lead us, He gives us something for free.

We get eternal life. Eternal life means we get to live forever and ever in heaven when we die.

You see, to be *perfectly* fair, eternal life is only for people who never sin. To be in God's presence, we need to be completely without fault.

The Bible sums up our problem in Romans 3:23 (NIV): *For all have sinned and fallen short of the glory of God.* ALL of us have sinned. ALL of us have fallen short and are not really good enough for heaven. Instead, we have a price to pay for our sin: death.

I'm sure you are familiar with the word "consequence." It's the word used to describe the results of our actions. There are good consequences and bad ones. If we do something wrong, like cheating on a test, we have to pay the consequences like maybe failing that test.

There's a verse in the Bible that tells what the consequences of sin are:

Romans 6:23 (NIV): *For the wages of sin is death…*

That means an eternity without God.

There's a second half to that verse though: *...but the gift of God is eternal life in Christ Jesus our Lord.*

How does this gift work? Since we *all* have sinned, we *all* need to pay the consequences. But God couldn't stand the thought of being apart from us for eternity, so He decided to pay the consequences FOR us.

The Bible says, *God so loved the world that he gave his one and only Son, that whoever believes in him shall not perish but have eternal life* (John 3:16, NIV).

God sent His Son, Jesus, to pay for our consequences by dying on a cross. His death paid the price for our sin, and it is God's great GIFT to us. This is grace. We don't deserve for someone else to pay for our sins, but God did it anyway. All we need to do is accept that gift and allow God to lead our lives.

Have you accepted God's gift of grace yet? Are you following Him and serving Him?

If you haven't accepted God's gift yet and you would like to, ask your leader to help you pray and ask for it. If you have accepted this gift, you have some really good news to share with your friends and family about God!

(Be open to your bakers being interested in accepting Jesus into their hearts. If you aren't familiar with how to share the Gospel message, see the lesson on "Fisher's of Men Oreo® Pops.")

Pray:

Spend some time thanking God for paying the price for your sins and making a way for you to spend eternity with Him in Heaven.

(You may want to make an extra batch of cookies or treats ahead of time to pull out and offer as a surprise bit of grace at this point!)

CHOCOLATE CHIP OATMEAL COOKIES
Theme: Keeping a pure heart

Today's lesson will focus on purity and the idea that just a little bit of sin separates us from God and can ruin our lives. These are basic (and very yummy!) chocolate chip oatmeal cookies. The most important part of the recipe today is the one, single raisin we will add at the end.

Make a point of adding it and enjoy all the "why" questions you will get about that one raisin.

I've recommended the use of a cookie scoop to portion out the cookies before baking. If you don't have one, you can certainly make these with a spoon, but the scoop is a kitchen tool you will love for years to come, and it will save you time.

To keep kids involved in the baking, allow them to measure the ingredients. Explain what it means to measure brown sugar "packed," or pressed down into the cup rather than loose. If needed, explain how to "cream" the butter and sugars together.

Prep Time: 20 minutes   ***Bake Time:*** 30 minutes

A few safety reminders:

- **Wash hands before beginning to bake, and after handling eggs.**
- **Tie hair back.**
- **Be careful with the oven, especially when removing the cookie sheets. Parchment paper can slide off if the sheets are tipped too far.**

Ingredients: (Makes 32-36 cookies)

- **1 cup margarine**
- **1 cup brown sugar (packed)**
- **1 cup granulated sugar**
- **2 eggs**
- **1 teaspoon vanilla extract**
- **2 cups flour**
- **1 teaspoon baking soda**
- **¾ teaspoon salt**
- **3 cups uncooked old-fashioned oatmeal**
- **2 cups chocolate chips**
- **One small box of raisins.**

Getting Started:

- Check your ingredient list to make sure you have everything you need.
- Preheat oven to 375° F.
- Cut parchment paper to fit each of your cookie sheets.

NOW, YOU ARE READY TO BAKE!

Directions:

- Add margarine, brown sugar, and granulated sugar to a large mixing bowl.
- Cream margarine and sugars together until smooth.
- Add eggs and vanilla extract and mix well.
- Add flour, soda, and salt. Mix until completely combined.
- Add chocolate chips and oatmeal.
- Mix all ingredients well.
- Scoop or spoon about 2-3 teaspoons of dough onto cookie sheets, leaving room for them to spread out as they bake.
- Bake at 375° F for 10-14 minutes. Remove from oven and slide parchment paper and cookies off sheet and onto counter to cool.

Lesson:

I hope you enjoyed making these cookies today! They smell wonderful, don't they? While they cool, I want to tell you a story.

I love animals. Do any of you have pets? When I was in college, I had a pet rabbit named Millie. She was the cutest thing. She was only half lop-eared, so one ear always stood up and the other flopped over.

Millie was litter box trained, so she spent her days hopping around my apartment, and when she needed to relieve herself, she would hop into her cage and use a litter box like a cat. Millie rarely had accidents, but occasionally a little round rabbit poop would get stuck on her fur, and it would end up somewhere on my apartment floor.

Every once in a while a friend would find one of these droppings on the floor and joke that I should collect them and make a "special" batch of chocolate chip cookies.

GROSS!

You are about to go and enjoy some cookies. Would you eat them if you knew that instead of chocolate chips we had added rabbit droppings?

Okay, let's say we added chocolate chips and all the other ingredients were fine, but we added just ONE rabbit dropping? Remember the raisin? Pretend that one raisin was not just a raisin…. Would you still eat the cookies? We mixed that raisin into the dough really well, and it touched a lot of other things.

One yucky addition to our cookies would have ruined the entire batch.

This is a lot like life.

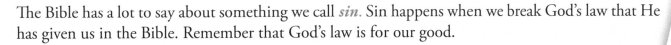

The Bible has a lot to say about something we call *sin*. Sin happens when we break God's law that He has given us in the Bible. Remember that God's law is for our good.

A lot of people think that if something is mostly good it is okay. Have you ever heard someone say,

> *"That was the best movie EVER. There was a ton of swearing, but it was such a good story!"*

Or

> *"I love that song! I know the lyrics are dirty, but I just listen to the music. They have a great guitar player!"*

That is just like saying, *"These are the best chocolate chip cookies ever! I know there's a little bit of poop in them, but it's only a little, and the chocolate chips are so good!"*

- Can you think of an example of a time when you accepted something as good even though there was some bad in it? (Allow a few minutes for kids to respond.)

Here's what the Bible says:

This is my prayer: that your love may abound more and more in knowledge and depth of insight, so that you may be able to discern what is best and may be pure and blameless for the day of Christ (Philippians 1:9-10, NIV).

We need to be able to discern (or figure out) what is good in life and what is not. Then we need to decide to fill up our lives with the good and block out the bad.

What are some good things to fill up our lives with? The Bible is the perfect place to start looking for that answer:

Finally, brothers and sisters, whatever is true, whatever is noble, whatever is right, whatever is pure, whatever is lovely, whatever is admirable—if anything is excellent or praiseworthy—think about such things (Philippians 4:8, NIV).

What are the opposites of these things? (Allow kids to answer, but be ready to help if they struggle with a few of these opposites.)

True: _____   Lovely: _____

Noble: _____   Admirable: _____

Right: _____   Excellent: _____

Pure: _____   Praiseworthy: _____

These opposites are a good starting point for recognizing things to avoid.

What happens when we pay attention to what we are allowing in our lives and block out the sinful things? Matthew 5:8 (NIV) tells us: *Blessed are the pure in heart, for they will see God.*

What do we do if we have already allowed impure things into our lives?

A famous king of the Bible, David, had that exact problem, and he prayed this prayer:

Create in me a clean heart, O God; and renew a right spirit within me (Psalm 51:10, KJV). God forgave him, and he was allowed a fresh start.

- Are there things you are allowing into your life that are displeasing to God?

- Are you willing to pray like David and ask for a fresh start?

- What are some ways you can keep your life pure?

It's time to enjoy some cookies together. When you find that raisin, remember what it *could have been,* and ask God to help you identify and get rid of the things that should not be in your life.

(If any of the kids feel like they should pray a prayer for forgiveness, you can stop and pray with them. You can pray David's prayer exactly if you want.)

Pray:

Close the session with prayer for an ability to recognize good and bad in life and for a desire to obey God in getting out the sinful things and deciding to keep a pure heart.

RASPBERRY BANANA TURNOVERS
Theme: The Fruit of the Spirit

These turnovers use an ingredient called puff pastry, and it is SO much fun! It is a special type of pastry that rises four to eight times as big as its original size. If you make a puff pastry from scratch, you roll a flour-based crust around a layer of butter and then turn it and roll it again, creating many layers of butter trapped between dough. When it bakes, that butter melts and creates steam. The steam causes pockets of air to form, creating a light and airy pastry. We are going to use a store-bought puff pastry to save time, but now you know how it works!

Remember to thaw out your puffed pastry before the kids arrive.

> **Prep Time:** 15 minutes **Bake Time:** 20-25 minutes

Ingredients: (Makes 8 large turnovers)

- One package of frozen puff pastry sheets, thawed
- One banana
- ½ cup raspberry preserves
- 1 cup powdered sugar
- 2-3 tablespoons milk
- 1 teaspoon vanilla

Directions:

- Preheat oven to 400° F.
- Cut banana into 16 slices.
- Gently unfold a sheet of pastry and use a knife to cut it evenly into 4 squares. Do this with both sheets.
- Take one pastry square, and spoon about a tablespoon of raspberry on it.
- Place 2 banana slices on top of the preserves and fold sheet over, diagonally.
- Use fingers to press edges together, take your time and press them *very* firmly together so there are no gaps.
- Use a fork to press edges together even more firmly (see photo).
- Cover large cookie sheets with parchment paper and carefully place each turnover on the parchment paper.
- Bake at 400° F for 20-25 minutes until golden brown.
- Remove from oven and allow turnovers to cool a bit. Don't be sad if some of them leaked a little; they will still be so yummy!
- Make glaze by combining powdered sugar, milk, and vanilla. Adjust the sugar amounts until you have a thick icing.
- Drizzle the icing over each turnover and gobble them up!

Lesson:

- What's your favorite kind of fruit?

This recipe calls for raspberries and bananas, but you could use lots of different types of fruit in these turnovers.

- If you could make any kind of turnovers, what combinations of fruit would you use?

- Have you ever been able to pick your own fruit off a tree or bush?

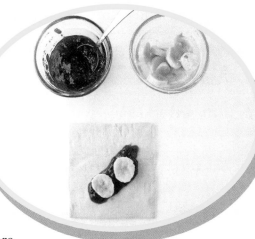

When I was growing up in Michigan, we had wild blackberries that grew in the forest behind our house. They were SO good, but blackberries grow on very prickly vines, and since they grew wild, all the vines were twisted together in big prickly piles. I remember putting on pants and a long-sleeved shirt to go picking in the hot July sun, but all the work was worth it when you had a big bowl of freshly washed berries to eat on the front porch swing.

There are easier fruits to pick than blackberries. Michigan is also known for its crops of sweet blueberries. All along Lake Michigan, where the soil is sandy, there are U-pick blueberry farms. My grandma used to take me, and the berries grow on tall bushes with no thorns—they just fall into your hands when you start to pick them.

Each type of fruit is unique. It requires certain temperatures, soils, and seasons. Some grows on trees, some on bushes, and some on short plants close to the ground. One thing is certain though—if you see oranges growing on a tree, you can say with confidence that you are looking at an orange tree.

How silly would it be if I had been picking blueberries with Grandma and pointed at that big blueberry bush and called it an apple tree? My grandma would have thought I was crazy. Blueberries don't grow on apple trees.

The Bible talks about this idea. In the book of Matthew, Jesus teaches His followers how to recognize people who aren't really following God, but just pretending to. He says, *By their fruit you will recognize them. Do people pick grapes from thorn bushes, or figs from thistles? Likewise, every good tree bears good fruit, but a bad tree bears bad fruit. A good tree cannot bear bad fruit, and a bad tree cannot bear good fruit* (Matthew 7:16-18, NIV).

When we decide to follow Jesus, we become a *Christian*—or a Christ follower.

If we don't really mean it when we say we will follow Him—if we just pretend to be good for certain people and hide who we really are—this will eventually show up with *bad fruit* like anger, gossip, bitterness, and jealousy.

If we truly decide to follow Him by learning more about Him, talking with Him in prayer, and obeying what He teaches us, we will produce good fruit.

The Bible tells us what we will produce in the book of Galatians. *The fruit of the Spirit is love, joy, peace, forbearance, kindness, goodness, faithfulness, gentleness and self-control. Against such things there is no law* (Galatians 5:22-23, NIV). This type of fruit is sometimes referred to as the **Fruit of the Spirit** because the only way you can produce this kind of fruit is to have God living inside of you, producing it for you.

Let's take a closer look at what the Fruit of the Spirit means:

Love: the kind of love that even loves enemies and people who hurt you.

Joy: a happiness because of Jesus—no matter our circumstances—good or bad.

Peace: an inner calm—even in crisis—that believes God is in control.

Patience: a willingness to wait for God's plans to unfold, even when we wish we had answers right now.

Kindness: watching out for others' needs and taking time to help or speak words of encouragement to them.

Goodness: keeping your distance from all that displeases God. A purity in actions and speech—not just once in awhile, but even when you're alone—not meant to please other people, but out of love for God.

Faithfulness: being a trustworthy person. A person you can count on to always show up and a person who keeps his or her word.

Gentleness: having a kind and healing approach to people, especially those who have been hurt by others' words or actions.

Self-control: controlling your decisions and actions in obedience to God's Word. This means saying no to things that God says will hurt you or others, and saying yes to things that are healthy and will help you and others grow in knowing God.

- How does your fruit look?

The good news is that you don't have to try very hard to make yourself have these fruits. A strawberry is produced by a healthy, watered, fertilized, strawberry plant. Likewise, these fruits are produced by a healthy, growing relationship with God. If you are already following God and growing in Him, maybe you can already see some of these fruits in your life. Maybe you really care about someone who's unpopular in your class. Maybe you really *want* to keep your heart and mind pure from dirty movies, music, and books. Maybe you are always looking for ways to help others.

- Can you think of some good fruit that is already growing in your life?

(Allow a few moments for kids to respond.)

Thank God for these things. They come from Him, not from your own efforts.

If you are like me, you also see some bad fruit still in your life. Maybe you are angry instead of loving, or terribly impatient. Maybe you don't keep your promises, or you use harsh words. That is because we are in the process of being transformed from a bad fruit tree into a good fruit tree.

The temptation is to try and fix these things ourselves, but since they are fruits, they are a result of loving God and seeking Him. When we see bad fruit, we need to ask ourselves if we are seeking God, listening to Him, and following His Word.

- Can you think of any bad fruit in your life?

(Be sensitive as kids respond. Some children may be experiencing the conviction of the Holy Spirit for the first time about some of the wrong things they have done.)

Pray:

Before we go and eat some of those yummy turnovers, let's ask God to help us produce good fruit, and then thank Him for the things He is already changing in us.

HOT CHOCOLATE POPS

Theme: Being genuine with God and each other

This recipe doesn't involve any baking at all, just a lot of melting and pouring. At the end, you will have yummy chocolate-covered marshmallows that melt in hot milk to make creamy hot chocolate!

Note: This is a messy *recipe. An incredibly fun and yummy* messy *recipe!*

The lesson will talk about the mess made when making these, so don't try to prevent the mess. Just enjoy it! One precaution you can take that will save you lots of time in cleanup is to put parchment or wax paper over the surface you intend to use. Then all the chocolate dribbles can be easily picked up and thrown away at the end.

> *Prep Time:* 50 minutes *Bake Time:* 0 minutes

Ingredients: (Makes 8 hot chocolate pops)

- **One bag of Wilton® candy melts in white chocolate**
- **One bag of Wilton® candy melts in milk (or dark) chocolate**
- **Marshmallows (4 to 8 of them)**
- **Dowels or popsicle sticks**
- **3 oz. disposable cups (both plastic and paper ones work)**
- **Milk (8 oz.) for each mug of cocoa**

Note: You can find the candy melts and sticks at an arts and crafts store like Michaels or JoAnns.

Instructions:

- Place ½ bag of milk (or dark) chocolate candy melts in a microwave-safe bowl.
- Melt candy melts in the microwave in 30-second increments, stirring between times until smooth.
- Spoon melted candy into a zip-top bag and seal tightly!
- Set 8 of the 3 oz. cups on a plate or tray that will fit into your refrigerator.

- Carefully clip a corner off the zip-top bag and squeeze about a teaspoon of chocolate candy melts into the bottom of each cup. Tap cup against counter to spread chocolate and remove bubbles.

- Place cups in the refrigerator for about 3-5 minutes, until chocolate is hard.

- Cut marshmallows in half (or you can leave them whole, if you like a lot of marshmallow in your cocoa).

- Place a dowel or popsicle stick into marshmallow as shown.

- Remove cups from the refrigerator.

- Melt all of the white chocolate candy melts in the same way you did the milk chocolate ones.

- Equally divide into the cups on top of hardened chocolate, and while it is still soft, press marshmallow into cup. (This will squeeze the white chocolate up along the sides of the cup.) Tap to remove bubbles.

- Refrigerate about 5-10 minutes until second layer is hard, and then add remaining chocolate candy melts over the top, completely covering marshmallow.

- Place cups in refrigerator for about 30 minutes to harden.

- To remove the pop from the cup, clip top of cup with scissors and tear it down the side.

- To eat pop: Use a BIG mug (16 oz.) and heat up about 8 oz. of milk in it. Place pop in hot milk and stir until smooth and creamy!

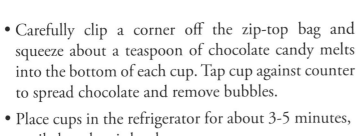

Lesson:

- What are the differences between what is real and what is fake?

  - How can you tell the difference?

  - What are some things that are easy to see the difference in?

(Allow some time for kids to respond.)

I think fake flowers ALWAYS look fake. I think "artificial sweetener" always tastes different than sugar.

- When is it hard to determine real from fake?

This might sound weird, but I think fake teeth are SO real looking! I have a crown, which is basically a fake tooth that replaces one that has cracked. I have a hard time remembering which one is fake because it looks so real.

I really love taking pictures of food, and I'm learning a lot about how really great food photographers get their pictures. Did you know that many food pictures you see in ads, menus, and billboards aren't even of real food?

Maple syrup is really hard to get a good picture of, so many food photographers use motor oil instead! If they are pouring that syrup over pancakes, it will soak right in, so they spray the pancakes with a fabric protecting spray first.

Another really hard-to-capture food photo is a bowl of something hot. Photographers might use wet cotton balls to help keep it steamy. They heat them up in the microwave and place them in the food where you can't see them.

Mashed potatoes in place of ice cream, white glue in place of milk with cereal, shoe polish to make steaks nice and brown.... You certainly wouldn't want to actually EAT a lot of the foods you see pictures of.

All of the pictures in this book are of real, edible foods; however, they aren't entirely honest pictures.

First, I didn't show you any of the behind-the-scenes mess I made! Did you make a mess, filling all those little cups with chocolate? I made a huge mess!

Second, I chose my BEST examples to photograph for you. Not all of my sticks were straight. I got chocolate all over some of them.

Third, I set up special lighting and reflecting boards to make the background white and the light perfectly reflected off each pop.

Fourth, I edited the photo on the computer to remove lines, whiten up the background, and make it look better.

I went to a lot of work to make these pops look perfect for you. The down side of this is that you might be REALLY disappointed that your pops don't look as "perfect" as mine.

This happens all the time. Have you ever seen a toy or game on TV that looked AMAZING—but when you got it and played it, you were bored? Advertising is very rarely genuine—because if it was, we wouldn't buy the product! Imagine a commercial that said something like: "Buy this game! It's super fun the first few times you play it, but then you'll never take it out of your closet again!"

Nobody would buy that game!

~~~~~~

This issue of being real, or genuine, instead of fake, is especially important with people. Sometimes it is really hard to know if someone is showing you his or her true, genuine self or being fake.

Have you ever thought someone was one way, only to find out later that it was all an act, and the person was really someone completely different? Have you ever pretended to be something that you aren't?

I think all of us are guilty of being fake sometimes, but the Bible calls us to be genuine when it comes to who we are.

There is a special word used to describe people who are fake about who they are: *hypocrite*.

A lot of people pretend to follow God. They think that as long as everyone around them believes they are following God it doesn't matter what they do in private or with people who don't care about God. These people are often referred to as hypocrites.

In the Bible, 1 John 1:6 (NIV) says: *If we claim to have fellowship with him and yet walk in the darkness, we lie and do not live out the truth.*

If we want to follow God, it's important that we follow Him even when others aren't watching, or when the people who *are* watching might make fun of us. Otherwise, we are lying and not living a truthful life.

If you have chosen to follow Christ, do you have a *real* relationship with Him, or are you faking it so others will think you are following when you really are not?

A good way to evaluate yourself is to look at your motives, or *why* you are doing something. Jesus talks about this in Matthew 6:1-18. He talks about giving, praying, and fasting. Then He says when we do those things to impress others, we are being hypocrites. We need to ask ourselves the question Paul asks in Galatians 1:10 (NIV), *Am I now trying to win the approval of human beings, or of God? Or am I trying to please people? If I were still trying to please people, I would not be a servant of Christ.*

- Are there things you do just to look good for others?

Another way Christians pretend is when we hide our sins and struggles and pretend we don't ever fail. We don't have to tell everyone in the world all of the things we mess up on and struggle with, but it is really helpful to have someone you trust to talk to about sin. It might be a parent or grandparent, or maybe a Christian teacher or Sunday school teacher.

Everyone sins and stumbles sometimes, and it's good to have someone older than you to talk to about it. I'm an adult, and I still have people in my life who I talk to about who I really am. It helps me grow when I am real with people, and I don't pretend to be doing better than I am.

The Bible says this about being real with people about our sin: *Therefore confess your sins to each other and pray for each other so that you may be healed. The prayer of a righteous person is powerful and effective* (James 5:16, NIV).

Following God and learning about how much He loves us is the most amazing journey on this planet, and we weren't made to take this journey alone. He gives us people all along the way to help us grow and obey, but if we aren't being real about who we are, we will hinder our own progress on the journey.

- What are some things you know in your heart about yourself that you aren't being real with people about?

- Can you think of someone you trust to talk with about these things?

One of the greatest benefits of being a genuine person is having real relationships with others and God.

- Can you think of someone who knows the real you and loves you in spite of your faults and mistakes?

(Allow some time for the kids to respond. Be sensitive and encouraging if kids feel comfortable sharing problem areas in their lives. Help them not to feel judged, but hopeful in finding solutions and living a real life with God and others.)

Those kinds of relationships are priceless, and the more genuine you are with others, the more of those relationships you will have.

When we are genuine, we will sometimes have messy kitchens and take bad pictures, but we will experience the peace that comes from not trying to pretend. We will also have a closer relationship with God and better relationships with those around us.

Pray:

Before we make and enjoy our hot chocolate, let's pray for God to help us to be real with Him and with the people around us.

CONFETTI MERINGUES
Theme: Being obedient

Today we are going to make something very unique in the kitchen.

Have you ever tried a meringue?

We are going to make cookies that are very similar to meringues. These cookies involve a special process that uses just the clear part (the white) of an egg.

We are going to use an electric mixer to beat egg whites until they become thick and form "peaks" when we lift the mixer away from them.

Before we begin this recipe, we need to talk about some rules that *have* to be followed when we beat egg whites. If we don't follow these rules, we will probably end up with soupy egg whites instead of light and fluffy ones.

The Rules:

1. Let eggs sit out at room temperature for at least 30 minutes before you use them.

   Make sure to set your eggs out ahead of time.

2. Make sure there is no oil or water in your bowl or on your beaters. Do not use a plastic bowl or anything with a surface that oils could stick to. I prefer glass bowls.

3. Make sure that ONLY the white (clear) part of the egg goes into the bowl. Just a tiny bit of yolk will prevent the egg whites from forming nice peaks.

NOW THAT YOU KNOW THE RULES, LET'S BAKE!

Prep Time: 10 minutes *Bake Time:* 45 minutes

Ingredients: (Makes about 24 medium cookies)

- **3 egg whites**
- **⅛ teaspoon salt**
- **3 ½ tablespoons of Jell-O® (any flavor, but not sugar free)**

You can make more than one flavor, but the bake time is quite long, so you might want to have the kids choose one flavor to make for this class and encourage them to try other flavors at home.

- **¾ cup sugar**
- **1 tablespoon vinegar**
- **Sprinkles for decorating**

Getting started:

- Check your ingredient list to make sure you have everything you need.
- Make sure you have the right equipment and that it is oil free.
- Cut parchment paper to fit on each cookie sheet.
- Preheat the oven to 250° F.

Step #1:

Practice separating eggs. Crack the egg over a bowl and gently tip the yolk back and forth between the two halves of the eggshell, letting the egg white pour into the bowl. You should be left with just an egg yolk in half of the shell. This takes a little practice. If you break the egg yolk before the white is separated out, you'll need to start over.

Make sure you have a lot of eggs on hand and that they are all at room temperature. Show the kids the technique first, and then let them practice over a small bowl. Every egg white that is successfully separated can be put with the others in a larger bowl for the recipe.

Step #2:

Add salt to the egg whites and use a mixer to beat on high until foamy.

Instruct the kids on how to use a mixer safely before letting them operate it.

Step #3:

Add Jell-O® and sugar as you beat the mixture.

Step #4:

Continue to beat mixture until it stands up in peaks when beaters are turned off and lifted away.

Step #5:

Add vinegar and gently mix until combined.

Step #6:

Spoon or scoop mixture to make small circles on parchment paper-covered cookie sheets.

I like using a cookie scoop for this part so all of them are the same shape and size, but you can use a spoon. Try to get all of the cookies onto 2 cookie sheets because the bake time is quite long, and you won't want to wait while a second batch bakes.

Step #7:

Sprinkle with decorations.

Step #8:

Bake at 250° F for 25 minutes and then turn oven off and allow cookies to sit in oven for an additional 20 minutes. Remove from oven and cool completely.

Lesson

(While cookies are baking and cooling, discuss the lesson. Let the kids answer and talk. Possible answers are provided so that you can direct the conversation along these lines.)

I hope you had a good time learning about meringues. Since they bake for a while, I'd like for you to think and talk about some questions while we wait.

- This recipe involves some pretty important rules about egg whites. Do you remember what they are? (Clean bowl, room temperature eggs, no yolks.)

- Who do you think made these rules? (Help them come to an understanding that these rules came from experience and experimentation with egg whites.)

- Why do you think the rules were made? (To save everyone from having to experiment, to help other people not to make the same mistakes, etc.)

- What might have happened if I hadn't told you the rules before we started? (The recipe might have not worked. Maybe we would have done the right things by chance, but our likelihood of success would decrease.)

- Who are some other people in your life who make rules? (parents, teachers, coaches, police, judges, pastors/Sunday school teachers, etc.)

- Why do you think they make rules for you? (They care about you; they want to protect you; they want you to succeed and avoid learning things the hard way, etc.)

Just like the rules in this recipe, the rules that people like parents, teachers, and coaches make in our lives are to help us do things right the first time. Often, the people making the rules have made mistakes before and hope to prevent us from making those same mistakes, or they are trying to protect us.

When I was little, my mom told my brother and me a story over and over to help us understand this idea:

Once there was a missionary family living in Africa. The father and mother had two kids, and they had a really important family rule: **When we ask you to do something, we want you to do it immediately, without complaining or asking questions.** One day, while they were out having a picnic lunch together, the kids were playing under a tree and suddenly their dad said, very quietly, "Kids, I want you to drop to the ground and slowly crawl toward me—*right now*." The kids knew the family rule, and even though what their dad was saying sounded crazy, they dropped to the ground and crawled toward him. When they got away from the tree, he hugged them and thanked them for obeying. He pointed back at the tree, and a huge poisonous snake was hanging just above where they had been playing. If they had ignored their dad or complained and argued, the snake might have attacked them.

The people who make rules in our lives deserve our respect and obedience, but rules made by people aren't always perfect rules. Sometimes people make mistakes or make rules that don't really matter. If you have ever gotten away with breaking a rule, you might even think most rules are dumb and need to be broken to see if anything bad really happens. You would be the person who goes home and tries this recipe with cold eggs, a plastic bowl, and egg yolks—just to see if it works!

In the Bible, Jesus tells a story about a man like that. He describes two men who built houses. A general rule for building a house is that it needs to stand on a firm and unmoving foundation. One of the men Jesus describes built his house on a strong rock foundation, while the other man decided to disregard that "silly" rule and built his house on a pile of sand. Then it began to rain. The winds blew hard against both houses, and what do you think happened? Of course, that house on the sand came crashing down.

Jesus says that the two men represent two types of people. The man who built his house on the rock is like a person who hears God's rules in the Bible and obeys them, while the man who built his house on the sand is like someone who hears those very same rules but decides to ignore them.

Of all the rules you will learn in your life, the ones in the Bible are the most important. Why? Because God is perfect and He loves you. This means His rules are perfect, and they are meant for your good. They are meant to protect you and guide you so that your life is built on rock instead of sand.

• Can you think of some of the rules in the Bible?

The first rules that most of us think of are the 10 commandments. That is a good place to start. Can you remember them all? They are found in Exodus 20. (You might want to look this up with them and talk about what each commandment means.)

It is very important to know God's rules. How do we know them? By reading the Bible and learning from people who teach us about the Bible.

There is something even more important than *knowing* God's rules: OBEYING them.

Remember the man who built his house on sand? He knew it was a bad idea, but he took a chance and went against the rules.

In the Bible, Jesus describes someone else who knows the rules but doesn't follow them: *Anyone who listens to the word but does not do what it says is like someone who looks at his face in a mirror and, after looking at himself, goes away and immediately forgets what he looks like* (James 1:23-24, NIV).

Can you imagine getting ready for school, looking up in the mirror, and seeing a huge blob of toothpaste on your chin? Now, imagine you look away for a minute and get distracted and FORGET what you looked like. You leave for school with toothpaste all over your face. How EMBARRASSING!

Jesus loves you more than anyone else on this earth loves you. He wants to have a relationship with you. He wants you to love Him back. That love between you and Jesus will help you obey His rules. Jesus says, *If you love me, keep my commands* (John 14:15, NIV).

Think about someone you really love and respect. Maybe it's a parent, grandparent, teacher, or coach. If that person set up a rule in your life, you would probably be glad to follow it, even if it was hard, because you love him or her. It's the same way with God. We follow His rules because we love Him, and we believe His rules are for our good.

Your cookies must be almost done. I think you are really going to like them. Many recipes use beaten egg whites, so I'm sure you will have a chance to use these rules again. I hope that each time you follow these rules in other recipes you are reminded of the perfect set of laws God has given us in the Bible.

Pray:

All of these verses were written by David, and they are all beautiful prayers to God about desiring to obey His word. (End your lesson with prayer and either read these verses together before you pray or ask the kids to read them as a prayer.)

I have hidden your word in my heart that I might not sin against you. Psalm 119:11 (NIV)

Give me understanding, so that I may keep your law and obey it with all my heart.
Psalm 119:34 (NIV)

I have kept my feet from every evil path so that I might obey your word.
Psalm 119:101 (NIV)

Tie-Dyed Cake
Theme: Being thankful

Have you ever made a tie-dyed shirt? It is fun to see the bright colors, and no two shirts ever look exactly alike. The recipe we are making today will show you how to make a fun rainbow-colored cake! When we slice it, it will look like it has been tye-dyed! I used all the colors of the rainbow, but you can choose whatever colors you want and make a totally unique and colorful cake.

Prep Time: 30 minutes **Bake Time:** 25 minutes **Frosting/Decorating Time:** 10 minutes

Remember to thaw your whipped topping before the kids arrive.

Ingredients: (Makes a 9-inch round, 2-layer cake)

- **One boxed white cake mix, plus eggs, water, and oil to make according to the box.**
- **Food coloring gels in Purple, Aqua, Green, Pink, Orange, and Yellow**
- **One tub vanilla frosting**
- **One tub whipped topping, thawed**
- **Colorful sprinkles**

Note: Food color gels can be found at any cake decorating store or arts and crafts store like Michaels or JoAnns. Gel colors will give you more vivid colors than liquid will.

Directions:

- Preheat oven to 350° F.
- Make cake mix according to the directions on the box.
- Grease two 9-inch round cake pans and place a circle of parchment paper in the bottom of each.
- Evenly divide batter into 6 small bowls (about 1 cup of batter in each).
- Add icing color gels to color each bowl of batter and mix well.
- Pour ½ of the purple batter in the center of one pan.

- Pour ½ of the blue batter into the center of the purple batter. (Adding the blue will push the purple toward the edges. You can tap the pan on the counter to help it spread if your batter is very thick.)

- Continue to pour ½ of each color batter into the center until each color has been used once.

- In second pan do the same, but reverse the color order.

- Bake at 350° F according to the directions on the box.

- Remove from oven and cool. Tip over onto a wire cake rack to finish cooling, and peel away the parchment paper from the bottom of each layer.

- Make frosting by mixing together the tub of vanilla frosting and the tub of whipped topping. Mix until smooth.

- When cake is cool, use a large serrated knife to carefully level off the tops of each cake layer. Place one layer, cut side up on a serving plate. Frost the top of this layer.

- Place the second layer on top, cut side down, and frost entire cake.

- Add sprinkles before serving.

Lesson:

- What are some things you are thankful for?

(Hand out a sheet of paper to each baker and set a timer for 2 minutes. Have them write as many things as they can that they are thankful for. Ask them to share those things out loud. At the bottom of the page, have them write how they feel.)

There's something strange about being grateful. It makes you happy!

Even if you are having a really bad day, spending some time thinking about all the things you are GLAD for makes your heart a little happier.

Play the following game with them:

We are going to play a game.

You have one minute to identify everything in this room that is blue.

(Wait a minute or two while the kids look around.)

Now close your eyes.

Without looking, tell me everything that is green.

You were so focused on the blue things in the room that you didn't even really see the green things!

This is something that happens in life all the time.

If we spend all of our time focused on problems and hardships, we will have a hard time seeing anything good in life at all, but once we start paying attention to the things God has blessed us with, we see the good in life more and more.

Being thankful can take an ordinary day and make it something beautiful.

Think about the cake we just made. If we hadn't added any color to it at all, it would be just another plain white cake. Nothing special, just white cake. Sometimes our days feel plain and ordinary. One way to add a little color is to take time to thank God for all the things He's given us.

- How do you think this works? (Let them discuss their ideas about this.)

Being thankful begins with understanding this verse from the Bible: *Every good and perfect gift is from above, coming down from the Father of the heavenly lights, who does not change like shifting shadows* (James 1:17, NIV).

Good things don't just happen. They come from God; they are His gift to us. Think about nature. God didn't have to make our planet beautiful. He made amazing things like sunsets and mountains, giraffes and oceans. Imagine a world without smells. After gym, that may be a good thing, but imagine not being able to smell the cake that is baking. We spend most of our days walking right by miracles and never noticing them.

(Talk about some of the things we enjoy every day that we take for granted.)

I love giving people gifts. One of my favorite times of the year is Christmas because it gives me a reason to surprise people with gifts I think they will enjoy. Giving gifts is my favorite way to show people that I love them.

A few years ago, my mom and I worked together on a gift for my dad and my brother, John. They both love golf, and the biggest golf tournament in the United States is called the Masters Tournament. Mom and I decided to surprise them with tickets to the Masters. The tickets were expensive, so we saved up. The tickets were also hard to find, and we spent a lot of time looking for them. We were afraid they would come in the mail when Dad or John were home, so we spent weeks racing to the mailbox looking for them. Christmas morning finally arrived, and we were SO excited. Dad and John opened the package and were SHOCKED. They both started laughing and thanking us and talking about how excited they were. Mom and I still remember how fun it was to get them that gift.

How do you think we would have felt if they had opened the gift, looked at the tickets, and started complaining that they were hungry for lunch? What if Dad had just sighed and started to tell us about his bad day at work the day before?

(Talk about how we might have felt. Has this ever happened in their lives? How did they feel?)

We do this to God all the time.

God gives us amazing gifts like food on our table, family, friends, sunshine, vacations, health…but we take those things for granted and complain, instead of saying thank you.

When this happens, we miss out on something really big. We miss out on seeing how much God loves us.

The Bible says, *God so loved the world that he gave His one and only Son, that whoever believes in him shall not perish, but have eternal life* (John 3:16, NIV). That's a lot of love!

• God has given us the greatest gift of all. He has given us eternal life through His son, Jesus. Why?

What does the first part of that verse say? Because He LOVES us.

When we take the time to recognize all God has given to us and when we see how much He loves us, it changes everything.

Suddenly, a life that seems plain and boring is full of color and design because the God who created the universe loves us and has a plan for you and me.

Pray:

As we enjoy our colorful cake together, let's spend time talking about the things that God has given us. Let's spend some time thanking Him for loving us and giving us so many good gifts, especially Jesus.

Enter his gates with thanksgiving and his courts with praise; give thanks to him and praise his name. Psalm 100:4 (NIV)

SOCCER CUTOUT COOKIES
Theme: Guarding your heart

This recipe makes chocolate cutout cookies. You can cut them into any shape you want using different cookie cutters, but today we are going to use a circle cutter and decorate them like soccer balls. We will be using a special icing called royal icing that gets very hard once it sits out for a little while.

The timing on this is dependent on how many kids you have helping. These times are an estimate.

> **Prep Time:** 35 minutes **Bake Time:** 10 minutes **Icing Time:** 35 minutes

Cookie Ingredients: (Makes 24-30 cookies)

- **2 sticks (1 cup) butter, softened**
- **1 ½ cups sugar**
- **2 eggs**
- **1 teaspoon vanilla extract**
- **⅔ cup unsweetened cocoa powder**
- **3 cups flour**
- **½ teaspoon salt**
- **½ teaspoon baking powder**

Icing Ingredients:

- **4 cups powdered sugar**
- **¾ cup water**
- **3 tablespoons of meringue powder**
- **½ teaspoon clear vanilla**
- **Black gel food coloring**

Note: Both the meringue powder and the gel food color can be found with cake-decorating supplies in arts and crafts stores and some grocery stores.

Getting Started:

- **Check your ingredient list to make sure you have everything you need.**
- **Preheat oven to 375° F.**
- **Cut parchment paper to fit each of your cookie sheets.**

NOW, YOU ARE READY TO BAKE!

Cookie Steps:

- Put butter, sugar, eggs, vanilla, and cocoa together in large mixing bowl.

- Blend on medium speed with a mixer until smooth.

- Gradually add dry ingredients and mix until smooth. (Turn off mixer and use clean hands at the end to knead dough into a soft ball.)

- Roll out cookie dough on a piece of parchment paper. If you roll it thick, the cookies will take a little longer to bake. Thin cookies will take a little less time.

- Cut into circles using a circle cookie cutter (I used a 3" one), and place on a parchment-lined baking sheet.

- Bake for 8 to 11 minutes until the edges are firm.

- Gently slide parchment paper and cookies together off of cookie sheet and onto a flat surface. Cool *completely* before moving—this allows the cookie to harden.

Icing steps:

- If you are working with several children, you might want to make up 2 "stations" for icing—each one with a bowl, a bag of black icing, toothpicks, and a damp paper towel. If you are baking with younger kids, help them with everything involving the black icing—and protect your countertops with parchment paper! Remember also that you don't have to decorate every cookie as a soccer ball. If it is taking too much time, just frost and sprinkle with fun team colors!

- While cookies cool, make icing by putting the powdered sugar, water, meringue powder, and vanilla into a mixing bowl and stirring well.

- If icing is too thick, you can add a little more water; if it is too thin, you can add more powdered sugar.

- Pour about ¼ of the icing into a separate little bowl.

- Add a little black food coloring gel to this smaller portion, being careful not to get it on the counters or yourself!

- Mix well, until all icing in the small bowl is a dark black color.

- Carefully spoon into a zip-top bag and zip it closed.

- Have toothpicks and a couple of damp paper towels ready to use in decorating.

- Use a knife to frost a cooled cookie with white icing.

- Cut a *small* tip off the black icing bag and carefully squeeze one black circle into the center of the cookie and then 5 black circles around the edges.

- Immediately (before the icing gets hard), use a tooth-pick to pull the edges of the center circle out toward each of the other 5 circles (see photos).

- Wipe the toothpick on a damp paper towel between each use to keep it clean.

- Start with one of the outside circles and use the tooth-pick to pull toward the 3 closest neighboring circles and then 2 times out toward the edge of the cookie. (You are making each circle into a pentagram by pulling the edges out).

- Once all circles have been pulled out with a tooth-pick, let the cookie harden.

- Make all of your cookies into soccer balls, or decorate some with sprinkles in your favorite team colors!

Lesson:

- How many of you have played soccer?

I have only played a few times in my life, but I've watched a lot of games, and I've noticed that there are specific positions on the team that have special jobs.

- Can you think of any of those positions and jobs?

(Give kids time to respond to the questions as you go through the lesson.)

There are two parts to a team, right? Offense and defense.

The offense has the job of scoring points in the game, and the defense has the job of preventing the other team from scoring points.

One of the defensive positions is the goalie, and I think it's the scariest position on the team. There you are, the only one protecting the goal from that ball flying in and scoring the other team a point.

- What do you think would happen if the goalie got bored and started texting friends?

- What if the goalie was afraid of the ball?

- What if the goalie just didn't care if his or her team lost?

- What is the goalie's only job?

We have a job that is very similar to a goalie's. According to God, we should be putting all of our attention, focus, and energy into guarding something. Proverbs 4:23 (NIV) says, *Above all else, guard your heart, for everything you do flows from it.*

Guard your heart.

- What do you think this means?

(Let the kids discuss this. They might get into a discussion about protecting your heart from people and not letting people get close. Try to redirect them to the idea that we are protecting our hearts from sin or things that might cause us to sin. This verse does not advocate the building up of walls between people for protection.)

When God talks about our heart, He is not talking about our physical heart but about our spiritual and personal well-being. We are taught to take good care of our bodies. We are taught to exercise and eat right and brush our teeth. We are also careful about our minds. We go to school and learn. We would hate for people to think we are dumb, so we try hard to keep our minds active and learning.

We are so busy taking care of our physical body and our mind that we ignore the one thing God says is the most important: our heart. In our heart, we can connect with God. It is here that we understand His words in the Bible. In our heart is our conscience—the Holy Spirit—that little voice that tells us right from wrong.

God is saying the most important thing we can do with our heart (*above all else*) is to guard it.

- What do you think God wants us to guard our hearts from?

- What happens when we don't guard our hearts?

(A good verse to share here if you have time is James 1:15 (NIV): *Then, after desire has conceived, it gives birth to sin; and sin, when it is full-grown, gives birth to death.*

You can talk about how we need to flee from temptation instead of letting it in, because if we let it in, temptation can cause us to sin and eventually causes pain, loss, and death. Fleeing from temptation is one way to protect our hearts.)

- What are some things that distract us from guarding our hearts?

A goalie has to be constantly aware of what is going on in the game. He or she can't take his or her eyes off the ball, and when it comes, the goalie has to react quickly and KEEP IT OUT. It would be pretty silly if a goalie saw a ball coming and said, "Hold on. I need to think about this for a minute and decide if I actually want to keep this ball out of the goal." That ball would be in the net before he or she even finished the sentence!

We need to know what is right and what is wrong, and when we see something wrong headed our way, we need to keep it out. The Bible has many verses that talk about the importance of keeping a pure heart.

(If you have time, let some of the kids read the verses from the Bible.)

Blessed are the pure in heart for they will see God. Matthew 5:8 (NIV)

Who may ascend into the hill of the Lord? Or who may stand in His holy place? He who has clean hands and a pure heart. Psalm 24:3-4 (NKJV)

I have hidden your word in my heart that I might not sin against you. Psalm 119:11 (NIV)

A soccer team isn't only about defense, though. It's not enough to just keep the other team from scoring. To win the game, you need an offense— you need a strategy for scoring points for your team.

The Bible has a lot of information in it about actions that make a difference for God in the world around us. These actions bring things like hope and peace to the people around us and are pleasing to God. Here are a few actions you can take to be on the "offense" for God:

Above all, love each other deeply, for love covers a multitude of sins. 1 Peter 4:8 (NIV)

Don't let anyone look down on you because you are young, but set an example for the believers in speech, in conduct, in love, in faith and in purity. 1 Timothy 4:12 (NIV)

Do everything without grumbling or arguing. Philippians 2:14 (NIV)

Children, obey your parents in the Lord, for this is right. Ephesians 6:1 (NIV)

• Which of these actions are you already taking in your life?

• Is there one you would be willing to add this week?

It can be really hard to recognize what is right and what is wrong in this world. The good news is that we have help. When we accept Jesus into our life, the Holy Spirit moves into our heart and starts to speak. He will help us tell if something should be *kept out*, and He will also remind us of what actions we need to be taking to *do right*.

Pray:

As you decorate and enjoy your cookies together, think about how you are doing both offensively and defensively for God. Ask God to help you see opportunities to both guard your heart and take action in the world around you.

FISHERS OF MEN OREO® POPS
Theme: Sharing your faith

These candy melt-coverd Oreo® pops are so much fun to decorate!
Once you learn how to make them, you can create so many other fun designs!

> **Prep Time:** 50 minutes **Bake Time:** 0 minutes

Ingredients: (Makes 24 Oreo® Pops)

- **One package of Double Stuff Oreos®**
- **2 (12 oz.) bags of Wiltons® candy melts in light blue**
- **1 (12 oz.) bag of Wiltons® candy melts in white (optional)**
- **24 lollipop sticks**
- **24 goldfish crackers**
- **¼ cup brown sugar**
- **Small pearl decorating sprinkles**
- **Small treat bags and ribbon, if you want to package them to give away.**

Note: Candy melts, lollipop sticks, pearl sprinkles, and treat bags can all be found at an arts and crafts store like Michaels, JoAnns, or Hobby Lobby.

Directions:

- Carefully twist apart all Oreo® cookies. Do this slowly and gently, and expect that some will break. Those are the ones you can snack on while you work!

- Microwave about ½ cup white candy melts using a microwave-safe bowl for 30 seconds. I use white to match the white Oreo® filling. If you aren't particular about the inside of your Oreo® being blue, you can just melt a little of the blue to use inside.

- Stir and melt for another 30 seconds. Repeat this until the candy melts are melted and smooth.

- Use a lollipop stick to make an indentation in the white filling of an Oreo®.

- Dip the end of the stick into the candy melts, spread a little on top of the white filling, and then press the stick into the indentation.

- Place the top of the Oreo® back on and allow the candy melts to harden and cement the cookie back together with the stick inside. You can do all of these steps on a cookie sheet or large plate and put the Oreos® into the fridge for 5 minutes or so to harden them up fast.

- While you wait, melt your blue candy melts in the same manner as you melted the white, stirring until completely smooth.

- Once the cookies are firmly hardened back together, pick one up (using the stick) and dip it into the bowl of blue candy melts.

- Spoon candy melts over the top and sides.

- Gently lift the Oreo® out of the candy melts, and tap the stick on the side of the bowl to allow the excess melts to drip off.

- Slide the bottom of the Oreo® against the edge of the bowl to remove excess candy melts.

- Gently set the coated Oreo® on clean parchment or wax paper.

- Immediately, set a goldfish in the center of the cookie, sprinkle brown sugar at the bottom, and place little pearl "bubbles" over the goldfish. Use the photos to help you with decorating.

- Do this with each cookie and then allow them to harden completely.

- Serve as is, or package for giving away by sliding each cookie into a little treat bag and tying with a ribbon.

Lesson:

Every time I make these cookie treats I am reminded of this story in the Bible:

While walking by the Sea of Galilee, he [Jesus] saw two brothers, Simon (who is called Peter) and Andrew his brother, casting a net into the sea, for they were fishermen. And he said to them, "Follow me, and I will make you fishers of men." Immediately they left their nets and followed him.
Matthew 4:18-20 (ESV)

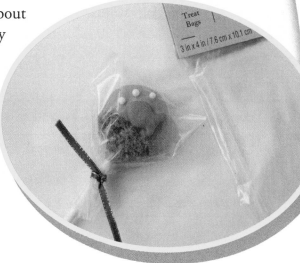

Jesus is just starting out on His mission to tell the world about who He is (the Son of God!). He is stopping along His way to choose people to help Him spread this good news. These people He is choosing will become the group of men known as the disciples.

Jesus is walking along the sea, and He sees two guys fishing with a big net. He tells them, "Follow me!" and then explains that He wants them to fish for something other than fish. He wants them to fish for *men*.

- What do you think this means?

- Have you ever been fishing?

The last time I went fishing, I was on the Amazon River with my friend Deb. We were taken out to fish for piranha. There's nothing quite as exciting as dropping a hook in the water and feeling that little tug on the line, knowing there's a PIRANHA on the other end! I caught 8 piranhas that night and learned how to take them off the hook VERY carefully to avoid those sharp teeth!

When Jesus says He wants to make Peter and Andrew into fishers of men, He is telling them He wants them to stop spending time hauling fish into a boat and start capturing people's hearts and minds for God instead.

- How did Peter and Andrew respond? (*Immediately they left their nets and followed Him.*)

If you spend some time reading in the Bible about Peter and Andrew, you will see that they became VERY good at teaching others about God and telling them the good news about Jesus. They became better at capturing men for God than they ever were at capturing fish.

Later in Jesus' life, He sends out an invitation for ALL people to follow Him and be fishers of men. That means me. That means YOU!

Jesus came and said to them, *All authority in heaven and on earth has been given to me. Go therefore and make disciples of all nations, baptizing them in the name of the Fathe and of the Son and of the Holy Spirit, teaching them to observe all that I have commanded you. And behold, I am with you always, to the end of the age.*
Matthew 28:18-20 (ESV)

These verses are called the *Great Commission*. The word commission can mean "instruction or task." So, this is God's Great Instruction or Great Task for us.

We need to go and tell people about Jesus and teach them to obey God in all that He has commanded.

- Have you ever told someone about Jesus before? What did you say?

(Give kids a chance to respond.)

There are two primary ways people will learn about God from us. They will learn by our actions and our words.

Actions:

People will look at what we do, and it will tell them what we believe about God.

For example, the Bible says people will know we follow God because of our love.

A new command I give you: Love one another. As I have loved you, so you must love one another. By this everyone will know that you are my disciples, if you love one another. John 13:34-35 (NIV)

- Are you good at loving people? Are there people you have a hard time loving?

- When you are angry or mean to people, how does this affect your message about God?

- Do you obey God's rules?

- When you cheat on a test or lie about something, how does this affect your message about God?

Words:

Our words can either do a lot of good or a lot of harm.

- Can you think of a time when someone said something to you that

    …encouraged you?

    …hurt you?

    …taught you?

We need to be careful that our words point people to God and don't discourage them or turn them away.

- Have you ever used words to tell people the good news about Jesus?

- How would you do that?

There are lots of ways to tell the story of Jesus, but here are the basics of the story with some Bible verses that are important to know:

God created us to be in a friendship with Him, and He loves us so much He even calls us His children.

See what kind of love the Father has given to us, that we should be called children of God; and so we are. 1 John 3:1 (ESV)

We broke that friendship by deciding we could do life on our own without following Him. (This is called "sin.")

For all have sinned and fall short of the glory of God. Romans 3:23 (NIV)

There is a cost to sin, just like there is a cost to breaking the law (a ticket or jail time). The cost of sin is death.

For the wages of sin is death, but the gift of God is eternal life in Christ Jesus our Lord. Romans 6:23 (NIV)

God decided (because He loves us so much!) to send His Son Jesus to become a human being like us and pay the price for ALL OF US, by dying for our sin.

But God shows his love for us in that while we were still sinners, Christ died for us. Romans 5:8 (ESV)

We can accept this payment for our sin, and this restores our friendship with God!

If you confess with your mouth that Jesus is Lord and believe in your heart that God raised him from the dead, you will be saved. Romans 10:9 (ESV)

The second part of Romans 10:9 reminds us that not only did Jesus die for us, but He rose again. When He did that, He conquered sin and death (1 Corinthians 15:56-57). This gives Him the authority to lead us. We need to choose not to do life on our own anymore, but let God lead us and follow His commands in the Bible.

If you love me, you will keep my commandments. John 14:15 (ESV)

When we do this, we live a life that shows others that God loves them, and we are given eternal life with God in heaven.

For God so loved the world, that he gave his only Son, that whoever believes in him should not perish but have eternal life. John 3:16 (ESV)

If this story is new to you, maybe you need to make the decision to accept Jesus' payment for your sins and choose to follow God. Talk to your leader about making this decision.

If you have already heard about and accepted the good news of Jesus, He is calling you, just like He called Peter and James: *Follow me, and I will make you fishers of men* (Matthew 4:19, ESV).

- Will you choose to follow Him?

- Will you start to capture people's hearts and minds for God, using your words and your actions?

(Allow time for the children to respond. Jesus may be speaking to some of their hearts for the first time, or they may have more questions about what they have learned.)

One way to begin is to memorize some of the verses we mentioned in this lesson. Maybe you can come up with a way to memorize them together!

(The scriptures are located in the back of the book if you would like to photocopy them and hand them out to the kids.)

Pray:

Let's spend some time praying together that we will be obedient to God in telling everyone we know about Jesus and how He made it possible for us to have a relationship with God.

CINNAMON UPSIDE-DOWN CAKES

Theme: Living life "upside down" for God

These fun little cakes are made in a special way—upside down! When they are finished, they are yummy yellow mini-cakes with a crunchy cinnamon and nut topping!

> **Prep Time:** 15 minutes **Bake Time:** 20 minutes

Ingredients: (Makes 24 mini-cakes)

- **2 cups brown sugar**
- **½ cup butter (melted)**
- **2 tablespoons cinnamon**
- **36 pecan halves (optional)**
- **One boxed yellow cake mix**
- **Water, oil, and eggs to make mix according to box**
- **1 cup powdered sugar**
- **1-2 tablespoons milk**
- **½ teaspoon vanilla**

Directions:

- Preheat oven to 350° F.
- Spray a muffin tin with non-stick cooking spray.
- Place brown sugar, cinnamon, and melted butter into a small bowl and mix until well combined.
- Spoon mixture evenly into all 12 cups of the muffin tin.
- Use clean fingers to press sugar mixture flat into the bottom of each cup.
- Place 3 pecans on top of sugar.
- Make cake mix according to box instructions.
- Scoop batter over the top of sugar and pecans. Fill each cup about ⅔ full.
- Bake at 350° F for 18-20 minutes.
- Remove from oven and quickly run a small knife around the edge of each cup.

- Place a wire cake rack on top of the muffin tin and (using oven mitts!) flip the pan and rack over so that cakes are upside down on the rack.

- Gently lift the muffin tin up and allow the cakes to pop out. Some sugar will remain in the bottom of each cup, which is fine.

Note: It is important to do this step right away while the cakes are still hot and not stuck to the pan. Use supervision if you let the kids do this step, as the pan can be awkward and hot.

- While cakes cool, make a glaze by mixing milk, vanilla, and powdered sugar together in a small bowl. Add milk or powdered sugar to make glaze a thick frosting consistency—not very runny.

- Spoon glaze into a small zip-top bag and seal the top.

- Use scissors to clip a small corner off and pipe glaze back and forth over the top of each little cake.

Lesson:

Have you ever looked at things upside down before?

Discuss how they did this. Did you stand on your head? Hang upside down? Ride a roller coaster?

Isn't it funny how things you see every day look completely different upside down?

These little cakes are different from other cakes because we put them together in a different order than a normal cake. Usually, you put the cake batter in and THEN the toppings. (That's why they call them TOPpings!) These cakes started with the toppings on the bottom, and the cake batter on top!

Did you know that when Jesus came to earth as a man He turned things upside down? He said things that really upset people because He didn't try to fit in or be accepted. He stayed true to who He was and what His Father asked Him to do. He said words that turned things upside down. In fact, *He* was upside down in that He wasn't ANYTHING like what they expected!

> People expected the Messiah to be rich. Jesus was born into a poor family.
>
> People expected Jesus would take over the government and bring change. Jesus died on a cross to bring us life instead.
>
> People expected Jesus to praise the pious church leaders. Jesus sternly scolded them and spent His time with "sinners."

One story from Jesus' life stands out to me as totally upside down, and it talks about something that is upside down in today's world too.

In Mark 9:33-35 (NIV), Jesus and the disciples are traveling along the road and some of the disciples begin to argue. When they arrive at their destination, Jesus asks them about it:

They came to Capernaum. When he was in the house, he asked them, "What were you arguing about on the road?" But they kept quiet because on the way they had argued about who was the greatest.

Sitting down, Jesus called the Twelve and said, "Anyone who wants to be first must be the very last, and the servant of all."

- What do you think Jesus means?

(Allow time for the kids to respond to the questions.)

- Can you think of anyone in your life who is concerned with being the greatest?

- Have you ever wanted to be the greatest? The most popular, the smartest, the best player on the team?

You might decide that to be popular you need to make fun of others to make yourself look better.

You might decide that to look smarter than others you need to use big words or pretend you know things that you don't.

You might decide that to be the best player on the team you need to hog the ball so you make all the big plays.

Let's be honest. Most of the time those things work. That's why people do them.

Jesus called His disciples—and us—to live life upside down.

He calls us to make friends with the unpopular and serve others without concern about what people will think of us.

He calls us to be honest about who we are and to help others understand and learn things—even if it means they get a better grade than us.

He calls us to be part of a team in which we help others to score points, and we don't take all the credit or praise.

In fact, He says that this is the *only* way to become truly great in God's eyes.

- What do you think about this?

- Would you rather be great in God's eyes or in other people's eyes?

This is a hard question. Many kids (and adults!) would say other people's eyes if they were honest. (This would be a great time to talk about how people will come and go in our lives. I never see the friends I had in high school and college anymore, but God is still here! Let kids be honest without rebuking them. It's important that they have adults they can be real with.)

As you try to live faithfully for God, you will come across many, many things that seem upside down. Everyone in the world around you will think that one way is right, and you will know from God's Word that it is wrong.

- The real question is: Are you willing to live an upside-down life for God?

- Are you willing to take a chance that there is more hope, joy, and peace in putting others first and yourself second?

There IS. But you might not see it at the beginning.

Remember when we poured cake batter over the toppings? I've been baking for a long time, and the first time I made this recipe I thought, "Well *that* seems weird to do. I hope this works out!"

You made these cakes and followed my recipe because you trusted I knew what I was doing when I gave you directions—even when it didn't make sense.

The same is true with God. We follow His Word even when it seems upside down to us, because we trust Him. We trust that He knows the best way, and we choose to do things His way.

- Do you trust God?

- Are you willing to follow Him even when the path seems confusing?

- What are some specific ways that you could put others before yourself this week?

- What are some specific things you could do to serve people?

Pray:

Before we feast on cinnamon upside-down cakes, let's pray together that God will show us He is trustworthy and faithful. Now, ask God to show you ways to put others before yourself this week. Most importantly, let's ask Him to help us all to lead an upside-down life for Him.

Appendix A

This activity goes with Lesson 1: *Fudge Cupcakes with Buttercream Icing*.

Make a copy for each person in your class.

Instructions:

Taste each ingredient on this list. Then write one word to describe what you think of it. Be creative!

LIST OF INGREDIENTS:

Flour   _____

Sugar   _____

Cocoa Powder   _____

Salt   _____

Baking Soda   _____

White Vinegar   _____

Vanilla   _____

Vegetable Oil   _____

Water   _____

Appendix B

This Scripture passage, 1 Corinthians 12:14-27 (NIV), goes with Lesson 3: *Cinnamon Cheesecake Sundaes*.

Photocopy and cut the sections apart. Give each child a section to read aloud. The sections are numbered so the children will know when it is their turn. If there are fewer children, then a child can read two of them or the leader can read the extras.

1) Even so the body is not made up of one part but of many. Now if the foot should say, "Because I am not a hand, I do not belong to the body," it would not for that reason stop being part of the body.

2) And if the ear should say, "Because I am not an eye, I do not belong to the body," it would not for that reason stop being part of the body. If the whole body were an eye, where would the sense of hearing be? If the whole body were an ear, where would the sense of smell be?

3) But in fact God has placed the parts in the body, every one of them, just as he wanted them to be. If they were all one part, where would the body be? As it is, there are many parts, but one body.

4) The eye cannot say to the hand, "I don't need you!" And the head cannot say to the feet, "I don't need you!"

5) On the contrary, those parts of the body that seem to be weaker are indispensable, and the parts that we think are less honorable we treat with special honor.

6) And the parts that are unpresentable are treated with special modesty, while our presentable parts need no special treatment.

7) But God has put the body together, giving greater honor to the parts that lacked it, so that there should be no division in the body, but that its parts should have equal concern for each other.

8) If one part suffers, every part suffers with it; if one part is honored, every part rejoices with it. Now you are the body of Christ, and each one of you is a part of it.

Appendix C

This information goes with Lesson 11: *Fishers of Men Oreo® Pops.* Photocopy and hand out to each child in your class. Not only will this help them to remember the story of Jesus themselves, but will be a resource for when they want to share with their friends and family also.

How to Share the Story of Jesus

Here are the basics of the story with some Bible verses that are important to know:

God created us to be in a friendship with Him, and He loves us so much He even calls us His children.

See what kind of love the Father has given to us, that we should be called children of God; and so we are. 1 John 3:1 (ESV)

We broke that friendship by deciding we could do life on our own without following Him. (This is called "sin.")

For all have sinned and fall short of the glory of God. Romans 3:23 (NIV)

There is a cost to sin, just like there is a cost to breaking the law (a ticket or jail time). The cost of sin is death.

For the wages of sin is death, but the gift of God is eternal life in Christ Jesus our Lord. Romans 6:23 (NIV)

God decided (because He loves us so much!) to send His Son Jesus to become a human being like us and pay the price for ALL OF US, by dying for our sin.

But God shows his love for us in that while we were still sinners, Christ died for us. Romans 5:8 (ESV)

We can accept this payment for our sin, and this restores our friendship with God!

If you confess with your mouth that Jesus is Lord and believe in your heart that God raised him from the dead, you will be saved. Romans 10:9 (ESV)

The second part of Romans 10:9 reminds us that not only did Jesus die for us, but He rose again. When He did that, He conquered sin and death (1 Corinthians 15:56-57). This gives Him the authority to lead us. We need to choose not to do life on our own anymore, but let God lead us and follow His commands in the Bible.

If you love me, you will keep my commandments. John 14:15 (ESV)

When we do this, we live a life that shows others that God loves them, and we are given eternal life with God in heaven.

For God so loved the world, that he gave his only Son, that whoever believes in him should not perish but have eternal life. John 3:16 (ESV)

If this story is new to you, maybe you need to make the decision to accept Jesus' payment for your sins and choose to follow God.

If you have already heard about and accepted the good news of Jesus, He is calling you, just like He called Peter and James: *Follow me, and I will make you fishers of men* (Matthew 4:19, ESV).

WILL YOU CHOOSE TO FOLLOW HIM?

Notes: